A guide to making big shifts

BREAK THROUGHS ARE EVERY WHERE

Curtis Carnes

Author's Note: The Breakthrough Circle was adapted from Mike Breen's Learning Circle with permission. Some names have been changed for privacy.

Book design by Steve Shuman

1st edition 2024

For Jay

TABLE OF CONTENTS

BREAKTHROUGHS ARE EVERYWHERE
—

BREAKTHROUGHS ARE IN THIS BOOK. They
are in conversations with your team. They are at your
off-site meetings. They are in discussions with your
partner. They are in your work. They are in your emotions. They are in your body. They are found over cups
of coffee. While you are on a hike. When you are negotiating a deal. When you are forming a strategy. When
you are considering your next move. Breakthroughs
are everywhere.

You are missing them because you have believed
this myth:

BREAKTHROUGHS ARE RARE

When you believe that myth, your eyes are closed to
the reality of breakthroughs. It keeps you from creating
your own map. It causes you to settle for maps others
offer you. It keeps you from presenting that new idea
that demands attention. It makes you believe you are
supposed to be here, not there. It keeps you in cycles of
interacting with others you know you should stop. It
stifles courage. It restricts freedom. It frustrates you. It
makes you feel that you have to take what you can get.
It makes you stingy. It causes you to rehearse the same
old stories you tell yourself. It keeps you from impact-
ing the world and getting paid for it.

I want to shatter this myth so you can experience breakthroughs every day.

IT'S NOT A LIE IF YOU BELIEVE IT

In an episode of *Seinfeld*, Jerry agrees to take a lie detector test to prove he's not an avid fan of the soap opera *Melrose Place*. The problem is that he watches the show all the time.

He brings in George, a serial liar, to help him before the test. George looks Jerry straight in the eye and says, "It's not a lie if you believe it."

If you believe that breakthroughs are rare, it is your reality. It doesn't matter if you *know* it's a myth if you *believe* it. Your belief drives your behavior. Simply, if you believe breakthroughs are rare, you act like it. I am inviting you to believe something radically different.

BREAKTHROUGHS ARE EVERYWHERE

Once you believe that breakthroughs are everywhere, making discoveries about your work, life, and relationships can become a normal part of your life. Acting on them would be, too. You would start creating your own way forward and inviting others to join you. You'd present that new idea or product. Start that venture. Take that risk. Have that conversation. Display courage. Receive from others. Be generous. Know your value. Be you. Feel free. Believe *you* can. Do *it*, whatever *it* is!

Part One

DEMYSTIFYING BREAKTHROUGH

I want to remove the mystery of breakthroughs by introducing the Breakthrough Equation and Breakthrough Circle, which will help you experience them every day.

Chapter 1

THE BREAKTHROUGH EQUATION
—

A BREAKTHROUGH IS A TRAJECTORY SHIFT IN YOUR LIFE. I want you to experience this. Not just once, but all the time. Here's how Sue describes her experience:

"I am a different person. I often wonder, 'Who is this new Sue?' Others are noticing, too. People I work with approach me and say, 'Who are you?' I would not be the leader I am today without [these breakthroughs]. I have found my voice. I believe my thoughts matter and need to be heard. I found courage. I am courageous. I am brave. This courage extended into my marriage and my relationships. I have surrendered my fears. I have strengthened my identity and feel like I have entered a new season, both personally and professionally. I don't think I have figured it out, but I am different. When I started this [journey], I was wearing a backpack full of rocks. I have flung all those rocks out of my backpack!'"

We'll learn more about Sue in a bit, but for now, I want you to see what's possible. The change that's waiting for you. A life full of breakthroughs is within your reach. I tell clients that all external outcomes begin with internal shifts. It starts with belief.

STEP 1: BELIEVE IT

The first step to making breakthroughs a regular and expected part of your life is believing *that breakthroughs can be a regular and expected part of your life.* The number of breakthroughs you experience will never exceed the number of breakthroughs you believe are available to you.

When breakthroughs seem rare, it's like finding a needle in a haystack. You're anxious. You're overwhelmed. You spin your wheels. You take the path of least resistance. You tell yourself that this is just the way it is.

When you believe breakthroughs are everywhere, you are full of anticipation. Take my young son, for example; you should see the huge smile on his face when he is hunting for easter eggs at my mother-in-law's house. She fills multiple garbage bags full of Easter eggs. In the past, 13 grandkids went looking for eggs; now, it's just him. The number of eggs has stayed the same—hundreds of eggs scattered everywhere—yet he's the only one looking.

When breakthroughs feel like that, you're running! You are full of energy and excitement. You're exploring everywhere because your breakthroughs are right there for the taking. There are as many as you are willing to grasp.

A breakthrough hunt is happening right now, and you're invited. Breakthroughs are everywhere, all around you. All you have to do is join in.

No one has told you to stop looking for breakthroughs. Breakthroughs are right there for the taking, and you can have as many as you are willing to grab. Will you join in?

STEP 2: JOIN IN

The most common reasons you stop looking for breakthroughs are the same reasons you stop looking for Easter eggs.

- I'm too old for this.
- What will people think?
- I'm not supposed to.
- It is something you pretend to do a few times a year. Then you get back to reality.
- I need to follow the rules.
- That's for other people.
- Fear.
- It's not realistic.

No wonder you feel like breakthroughs are rare. But I have good news for you!

- You are never too old for this!
- When you join in, it encourages others to do so!
- You're supposed to!
- Breakthroughs can be your reality!
- There are no rules against breakthrough!
- Breakthroughs are for you!
- There's no need to fear!
- It can be your life!

A breakthrough hunt is happening right now. Will you choose to join in?

STEP 3: EXPERIENCE BREAKTHROUGH

It's entirely up to you whether you will experience a breakthrough. If you decide to join in, you can experience breakthroughs! From over a decade of coaching leaders, individually and in groups, I have distilled how to unlock breakthroughs. It is called the Breakthrough Equation:

DISCOVERY x ACTION = BREAKTHROUGH

It's simple. Make discoveries. Take action. Experience breakthroughs. Period. Nothing more, nothing less.

Breakthroughs come in all shapes and sizes. They can be small, large, and everywhere in between. But they always consist of two things: Discovery and Action. You need both. One won't do.

DISCOVERY ≠ BREAKTHROUGH

Elementary school taught us that anything multiplied by zero is zero. If you discovered the new product would be a game changer in your industry and took no action, you'd have no breakthrough. You would have no breakthrough if you found a limiting belief holding you back and made no effort to reframe the narrative. You'd have no trajectory shift if you discovered what would make your business thrive for the next decade and took zero action. Nothing will change if you figure out what would take your relationship with your partner to the next level and don't act on it. Discovery alone does not lead to breakthroughs.

Making discoveries feels meaningful! And it should. I've seen others make critical discoveries that lead to significant breakthroughs. But having a discovery alone isn't enough. Without action, discovery is like an unlit matchstick—full of potential but not serving its purpose. It's easy to confuse the act of discovery with a breakthrough because it's exciting to have a eureka moment.

I love making discoveries. I love talking about them. I feel impressed with myself when I do. Especially when everyone is nodding their head. Yet, the discovery itself is not a breakthrough.

Some of us have a cathartic experience making and talking about our discoveries. We use this to absolve ourselves from action. We must remind ourselves that Discovery ≠ Breakthrough.

ACTION ≠ BREAKTHROUGH

Action alone does not lead to a breakthrough. It sure makes you busy! Yet busyness does not mean you are making a breakthrough. Just because you are moving doesn't mean you are any closer to where you want to go.

Action is misleading because it *feels like you are doing something.* And you like that feeling. Checking emails. Making calls. Making sure we are following the rules. But if your actions don't flow from genuine discovery, it won't get you far.

If you don't watch yourself closely, your actions can easily come from a desire to prove yourself or to fit in. Your actions may be coming from a place of fear or scarcity. Your actions may come from a limiting or false belief about yourself, your relationships, or your work. If you feel like you are going nowhere fast, ask yourself what's motivating your actions.

When your actions come from genuine discovery, you experience breakthroughs.

DISCOVERY x ACTION = BREAKTHROUGH

That's it! Make a discovery. Take action. Experience breakthrough. The bigger the discovery and more courageous the action, the more significant the break-through. Make it a lifestyle, and your life will go from trajectory 1 to trajectory 2.

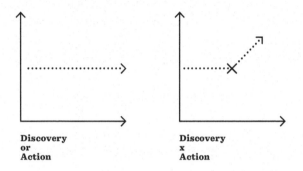

Discovery
or
Action

Discovery
x
Action

MY TRAJECTORY SHIFT

I sensed that I was in a season where it was time to go from *Curtis v3.0* to *Curtis v4.0*. Over the last five years, I have experienced professional, emotional, spiritual, personal, and relational breakthroughs. I knew it was culminating in one big trajectory shift. I was open and looking for discoveries. As I surveyed my life and looked to my future, I processed these two questions: Who am I? And where do I want to go?

I was challenged to describe myself in two words. It took me a month to discover them (actually a decade!). My two words are *energizing breakthrough*. I deeply resonate with them. I am a high-energy, direct person who feels alive when I am energizing breakthroughs in individuals, groups, and organizations. When I landed on these two words, I had that feeling you have when you put the last piece of a puzzle in place. My past clicked into place at that moment, and my future was clear. This discovery was a culmination of other discoveries and breakthroughs along the way. It led me to take a courageous step.

I left my job, where I enjoyed four weeks of vacation and a stable income, to go full-time into coaching to energize breakthroughs in individuals, groups, and organizations. Did I tell you we were a single-income family? It took a massive act of courage. I remember someone close to me asking, "How is it going telling everyone?" Without thinking, I blurted out, "The hardest conversation was the one I had with myself. After that, telling everyone else became easy." I faced my fears and stepped out of the boat.

I chose to believe, join in, and experience breakthroughs. Will you?

Believe. Join in. Experience breakthroughs. Not once, but all the time. Now, let's look at a proven tool that has led to breakthroughs for me and countless others.

Chapter 2

NAVIGATING THE BREAKTHROUGH CIRCLE

—

IMAGINE WHAT YOUR LIFE WOULD BE LIKE IF YOU WERE EXPERIENCING BREAK-THROUGHS EVERY DAY. You'd be making regular discoveries and taking consistent action. You'd have the self-awareness to discover what's truly important and the courage to focus exclusively on that. You'd take responsibility for your life rather than letting life happen to you. You'd show up as your authentic self at work and in your closest relationships. You'd tell yourself stories that reinforce the directions you feel compelled to go while discarding stories that no longer serve you.

You'd behave as if there is a surplus of resources, relationships, and opportunities out there for you. You'd operate from freedom rather than be driven by low-grade anxiety. You'd be generous because there is so much to go around. You'd speak up because what you have to say needs to be heard. You'd listen more because you don't need to prove yourself. You would let go of the things holding you back and grab onto the things that propel you forward.

The Breakthrough Circle is a simple tool that converts inflection points into concrete personal and professional breakthroughs. Countless people have used it. Now it's your turn. The reason why it's so impactful is because it's clear, it's repeatable, and it works.

The Breakthrough Circle

—

INFLECTION POINT

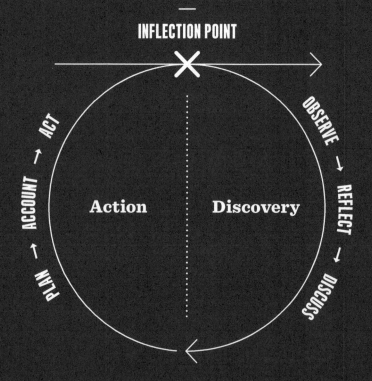

INFLECTION POINT

All breakthroughs begin with an inflection point. An inflection point is a "moment when change *may* occur." The keyword in that sentence is *may*. An inflection point contains a potential breakthrough. Whether it occurs is up to you. You must decide to take it full circle. An inflection point is a *moment* where you have the opportunity to make a discovery and take action.

Here's a small sample of potential inflection points:
- You have a conversation with a colleague where you land on the product or service that can move your company forward.
- You are reading a book and realize that shifting the way you approach work could drastically increase your impact.
- You have a special moment with your partner or child(ren) and wonder how to make more time for this.
- You realize that your scarcity mindset holds you back from taking appropriate risks.
- Your father passed away, and it has disrupted your work. You realize this is an opportunity to recalibrate your personal and professional life.
- You have a great workout and realize how much it helps you focus.
- You realize your annual review is coming up,

and you have never negotiated a salary.

· You stayed silent during a critical executive meeting when you had something significant to say and spent the rest of your day rehearsing what you could have said.

· You are butting heads with a colleague.

· You sense excitement in your team when you talk about that new idea.

· You are overwhelmed when you open up your calendar.

· You have a persistent desire for that new role.

· You notice that you are putting too much stock into what others say about you, good or bad.

· You sense a misalignment in your team.

· You feel incredibly energized when doing "X" and you wonder how you can do more of this.

This list is just a small sample. The point is this: Inflection points were everywhere. They are waiting just below the surface of your day. They are in your conversations with clients and families, the books you are reading, the emotions you are experiencing, during hikes in the park, while you are working, while you are playing with your children, and while you are brainstorming with colleagues.

Once you start looking, you will see them everywhere. For instance, my son and I started talking about getting a Jeep. All of a sudden, we were seeing Jeeps everywhere. If we saw one while driving, we would yell, "Jeep." I swear we were saying Jeep all the time. Did everyone in Cleveland suddenly decide to buy a Jeep? No! We see them everywhere now because we are looking for them.

Inflection points are no different. Once you are open to inflection points, you will see them everywhere. Here is the catch: You will never see them if you don't think they are anywhere. If you think they are everywhere, you will see them all the time.

Once you notice these moments, you can initiate the discovery process. Working your way around the circle turns an inflection point into a breakthrough.

DISCOVERY

Discovery happens when you *observe, reflect,* and *discuss* an inflection point.

Observe

The first step is to look. The number one reason you are not making discoveries about your life and work is that you are not looking for them! You are either too busy or too distracted. Or worse, you don't think that they are there.

An inflection point is a moment in time. An observation is when you become aware of that moment. Observing is all about making yourself aware of the inflection points that are all around you. Slow down and take time to look. Try it now. What's one inflection point that you have seen today?

The more you look, the more it changes how you see. You start to see inflection points everywhere, big and small. Observing goes from being a deliberate act to something you naturally do all the time. Chapter 3 is dedicated to this.

Reflect

Have you ever been excited about observing an inflection point in your life and work and then did nothing with it? I'm guilty of this. So is Jack. Jack is a business owner who is always on the move. He pulled out his phone and started scrolling through his calendar for me to see. "My life is out of control. Just look at my schedule." I hear this from most executives I coach. Jack just observed the pace of his work life. Jack has a choice. He can move on and keep running on the hampster wheel or take time to reflect.

What if Jack chose to reflect and ask himself:
· What is this discovery trying to tell me about my work?
· What is this discovery trying to say to me about myself?
· What makes me feel trapped in this hectic schedule?
· Why do I feel like I need to be in all these meetings?

- What am I clinging to that I need to let go of?
- What activities bring the most value?
- Where do I need to change my approach to work?
- How do I want to show up at work and home?

Even if Jack chose to answer just one of those questions, I'm sure he'd uncover something. Reflection unlocks observations. Reflection questions extract the value from observations. There are thousands of questions that you can ask. There are so many benefits to asking them.

Great questions help:
- Shift your perspective
- Gain clarity
- Surface desires and motivations
- Unlock insights
- Get below the surface
- Access the root causes
- Focus your energy
- Get you unstuck
- Instill courage
- Create new paths forward
- Uncover limiting beliefs and narratives
- Identify and maximize value
- Innovate

You can enjoy these benefits if you take the time to reflect.

Discuss

Sometimes, you do not believe you have a place to discuss the discoveries you are making in your personal and professional life. I've lost count of how often a client has said, "I haven't told this to anyone." They aren't confessing to affairs or embezzlement schemes! They are talking to me about their dreams, what would enable them to show up as their authentic self, what it would mean to live in freedom, or that one thing they have always wanted to do but still haven't done.

Just saying *it* out loud begins to set things in motion. Things start to happen when you let it out of the bag. Whatever *it* is. A client of mine is a successful business owner, and his business was the focus of our coaching relationship. He voiced his desire to become a part owner and integrator in other companies. It's been a five-year goal he never spoke about to anyone. Just the act of saying it out loud brought it closer to reality. We adjusted the focus of our coaching relationship because he shared his desire.

Then, he started to voice that desire to other business owners. He just had his proposal accepted to become a fractional integrator for a company. All this began to happen simply because he said it aloud. You will hear his whole story in Chapter 7.

What do you need to let out of the bag? It could be a unique way of focusing on a problem, the next iteration of your product or service, a new way to operate as a team, your dream job, or even a trip you always wanted to take. Voicing it is the first step in making it a reality. Tell someone!

Inviting others into your discoveries helps you go deeper. They might bring up an observation, insight, encouragement, or challenge that catapults your discovery forward. This is why a coach, friend, partner, or colleague who functions this way is worth their weight in gold.

Inviting others into your discoveries connects you to opportunities, resources, and people eager to support you. We will unpack this in Chapter 5. I've been connected to countless opportunities, resources, and people just because I invited others into the conversation about my discoveries. Whether it be a coach, a Breakthrough Group (see Chapter 8), a partner, a friend, or a colleague, find a safe person to invite into your discovery. When you do, things open up!

ACTION

The bottom of the circle is where I most often see the baton dropped. It's motivating to bring a new discovery to maturity. You even feel like you have made a breakthrough. You haven't. Remember, Discovery ≠ Breakthrough. I don't say this to squash anyone's motivation but so that you might harness it. Action is what turns discoveries into breakthroughs. Action involves three steps: *Plan, Account,* and *Act*.

Plan

Now what? The first half of the circle helps you answer the question: What discoveries am I making? The second half asks: "What am I going to do about it?" Now it's time to plan. Don't let your planning lag too far behind your discovery. You gain momentum when you plan action steps immediately. Here are my favorite questions to help you do this:

What's the best possible imagined future? This question is so important that it's a part of my intake for new clients. Casting an imagined future is motivating. Once you envision your future, you can begin to move towards it. What's your best possible imagined future?

What would you do if you were full of courage? I wrote this book as a response to this question. Here are some responses I have seen from clients:
- I'd negotiate my salary.
- I'd call the head of the league tomorrow morning and tell him my dream.
- I'd leave my corporate job and do my own thing.

- I'd write that letter to my son.
- I'd form an elite team around this initiative.
- I'd rediscover my voice and not allow anything to keep me from using it.
- I'd stop working at 5 pm.
- I'd start living more of my vision vs waiting until things are perfectly aligned.
- I'd completely reform my practice and how I communicate my offer.
- I'd change the way I engage with my spouse.
- I'd divest resources away from what has built our business over the last 20 years and invest in new markets.
- I'd change the way I process my anger.
- I'd have that conversation with someone.
- I'd focus all my energy on X.

This question provides a window into the type of action you should take. Now answer it for yourself!

What's your first/next step? If your discoveries are so significant, the planning process overwhelms you. If your action takes so much courage, it makes your feet tremble. If your desired future seems so remote that you don't know how to get there, try asking, "What's my next step?" You may not know step ten, so focus on the next step. Nothing makes you move like movement. So get moving! That's the only way to get where you want to go.

What action steps are you going to take? This is the essential question. Every question you can ask during the Plan stage of the Breakthrough Circle leads here. What are you going to do? The best action steps are concrete.

Generalized action steps get you nowhere. Concrete actions take you where you want to go. For instance, an executive client wanted to speak up with her authentic voice at work. She decided to use her authentic voice that week. If she had left our session with this generalized goal, it's unclear where that would go. I pressed her to be more specific. She decided to use *hesitation* as a trigger to speak up. Throughout her meetings and 1v1s, if she felt uneasy about saying something, she committed to leaning in and saying it. She did it. Now she's talking to the CEO every week!

Here's another way to say it: An action step is concrete if you can clearly visualize it happening. Bill owns a successful business and has been married for 15 years. Bill said, "I am realizing I need to start communicating more with my wife about what's happening inside me. I keep too much in, and it's been detrimental to our marriage. I will start sharing what's happening inside me with my wife." He made a significant discovery and committed to a generalized action. I asked, "What do you need to communicate to your spouse tonight?" He paused, then responded, "Tonight, I need to communicate the thoughts and feelings I experienced on vacation with my extended family last week." Now *that* is a concrete action step! You can instantly visualize that conversation happening. Visualization is a great litmus test for an action step.

Account

I am going to share with you the secret to accountability. It flips the common conception of it on its head. Rather than assign an accountability metric, *invite the other person to create it*. Here's the platinum question:

What question do you want me to ask you the next time we meet? This single question accomplishes so much. It makes the person responsible for the action responsible for the accountability metric. It creates ownership. It assumes follow-up. Since the person responsible for the action comes up with the question, the follow-up becomes effortless because the person told you what question to ask. Following the example above, I asked Bill, "What question do you want me to ask you the next time we meet?" He responded, "Ask me, 'How did the conversation with my wife go?'"

If you are working through the Breakthrough Circle by yourself, tweak the question this way: *What question do I want [insert person's name] to ask me the next time we connect?* Answer it, then communicate the question to her and when you want her to ask you. Self-generated accountability metrics propel breakthroughs.

Great accountability questions assume success. Too often, accountability questions are a version of "Did you do it or not?" A simple tweak can turn a poor question into a strong one. For instance:

Poor Question: Did I share the innovative idea with my business partner?

Strong Question: What came out of the conversation when I shared the innovative idea?

The former close-ended question is just a box to check. The latter open-ended question anticipates further discovery and action.

Act

Everything you have done with the Breakthrough Circle has led you to the moment where you do *it*. Whatever *it* is! You have observed and reflected on the discovery. You have invited others into the conversation. You created the plan and the accountability metric. Now you get to say I did *it*. This is the moment where the breakthrough occurs! The project launches. The book is written. The conversation happens. You hit your goals.

Here's the best part: Breakthroughs generate more breakthroughs! They are self-perpetuating! The more you have them, the more breakthroughs you can have. Breakthroughs create new inflection points, discoveries, and actions.

Do *it!* Whatever *it* is!

Part Two

—

THE FIVE BREAKTHROUGH SHIFTS

I have uncovered five shifts that will help you accelerate and increase your personal and professional breakthroughs. The first shift is going from information to discovery.

Chapter 3

FROM INFORMATION TO DISCOVERY
—

IF INFORMATION LED TO BREAKTHROUGHS, YOU WOULD THINK YOU WOULD BE MAKING BREAKTHROUGHS ALL THE TIME. You are drowning in content! It's everywhere you turn. Blogs, Twitter, podcasts, books (including this one!), conferences, Google, etc. If you want information, you can get it fast.

Our information age has perpetuated a myth: If you just had more information, you could make the breakthroughs you want in life and work. Many industries are built on this myth. We have the information, and you don't. Consume this information, and you will arrive. Are we there yet? Clearly not! Breakthroughs are the exception, not the norm.

We are asking for information to do what it was never intended to do for us. When information does not lead to breakthroughs, we throw up our hands and say, "Breakthrough is rare; it seldom happens, and you are lucky if it does." It's the equivalent of putting a paper recipe into an oven and expecting a pie to come out. Then complain to your family that this recipe never works!

The myth that information leads to breakthroughs is why you feel exhausted and believe they are rare.

This generates anxiety and stifles meaningful action. What if the problem is not the recipe but how you use it? The issue is not with breakthroughs but what you think it takes to achieve them.

CONFESSIONS OF AN INFORMATION ADDICT

Hello, my name is Curtis, and I am an information addict. *Step One: Admit you are an addict.* I have a confession to make: I love consuming information.

Consuming information:
· Makes me feel smart
· Makes me feel superior in a group when I am communicating said information
· Quells my low-grade anxiety
· Holds at bay the shame I feel from not taking action
· Gives the impression that I am making discoveries
· Temporarily makes me feel good about myself

Then, I look up from my book or take a break from my podcast. I realize that I invested thousands of dollars and three days away from my family to attend a conference simply to consume information. No meaningful action resulted from attending the conference. My work looks the same. I have not changed. I'm yet to experience a breakthrough. *This anxiety and exhaustion drive me back to take another "hit" of information to give me a boost.* So I start to search for the next conference I could attend or that next book.

The cycle continues. It's a merry-go-round that never stops. It's exhausting. It keeps you from significant shifts in your life. Even worse, it's been *normalized* in your life and work. Information consumption is expected and often celebrated. Yet, information promises you something that it cannot deliver. It's time to break the cycle for good.

As a recovering information addict, I am excited to tell you there is another way. Information alone will not help you get the life you're after; in fact, more info is what's keeping you stuck. Discovery is the gateway to the life you're after. When you make discovery the lens through which you view your life and work, everything changes!

CONVERSION

Over a decade ago, I was at a dead-end job. I was medicating myself with information. I was cruising through a master's program and consuming massive amounts of information. It *felt* like I was doing something, but it wasn't getting me anywhere. I was driven, but I knew firsthand that information was not propelling my vocation forward or helping my marriage. It did not significantly move my relationships forward. I felt stuck. Anyone who has subscribed to the information cycle knows what this feels like. You feel like you're trying so hard, yet you're not going anywhere. I knew from personal experience that information was not the way forward, but I didn't see another way. I was introduced to a version of the Breakthrough Circle and two questions:

1. *What discoveries are you making?*
2. *What are you doing about it?*

The circle and those two questions fundamentally changed my approach to life and work. It was a breath of fresh air. I started to process every area of my life through this lens: my work, leadership, marriage, family, faith, and emotional life. Discovery opened the door to breakthroughs in all these spaces for me, and it continues to do so. I have been around this circle countless times. What once was a breath of fresh air is now the air I breathe. It is my life. It is the journey I will always be on. I want you to join me.

REDISCOVERING DISCOVERY

A life of discovery may feel elusive, but it's not. You've done it before! It's hard-wired into you. You just need to rediscover it. I am confident in this because you were once a kid. Kids don't need to be taught discovery; it's what they do. You see this firsthand if you are a parent, grandparent, uncle, or aunt.

Our pantry has a basket of snacks on the lowest shelf that my younger son can have any time. The really *good snacks* he needs permission to have are on the top shelf. One day, I walked into the kitchen, and my son had a step stool pushed up against our pantry with red tongs in his hands, reaching at full extension for his favorite snack. Rather than asking himself, "What snack do I want from the basket on the bottom shelf?" My son asked, "How do I get my favorite snack that is out of my reach?"

You need to recover this mentality. You may be choosing from the bottom shelf when you could be reaching for the top shelf. Whether that's pursuing your dream vocation, courageously entering a new market, or having *that* conversation with your spouse or business partner.

Much of the friction you experience inside stems from going against your nature. It's time to rediscover discovery.

BELIEVE ITS THERE

Discovery is more than something you do; it's a belief. Discovery begins with the assumption that *there's something to be found.* There's always a reason to look when there is something to find! Even when you can't see it yet.

A client had a complicated working relationship with a direct report. Their communication style and approach to work were apples and oranges. It hindered their ability to reach their numbers. She needed to engage with him productively to meet their goals. She could have thrown her hands up and said it is what it is, but she didn't. Instead, she kept looking. She realized they overlapped in one area. They shared the same passion for their team's goals. She decided to be 100% goal-focused when engaging with him. It unlocked their relationship, and now they are exceeding their yearly targets. All because she remained steadfast in her belief that there was something to be found. She could have given up, but she didn't.

Discovery is fundamentally a belief. This belief gives you the confidence to look. It is only when you seek that you will find.

BE CURIOUS

You were born curious. When you were a kid, you explored everything. Through exploration, you gained awareness, insight, and shifts in perspective. You discovered new things about yourself, your world, and your place in it. This curiosity led you to discoveries.

You asked questions all the time until your parents got sick of you.

Why did you stop? Your upbringing taught you to value answers over questions. It turns out your upbringing was wrong! Answers don't lead to anything new, but questions do. It's time to be curious again. Start asking questions.

Let me introduce you to a client named Craig. Craig oversaw the large accounts for an international data processing company. A big client informed him that their services were not meeting their needs and they would terminate the relationship. He could have responded with answers, but he asked questions instead. He asked himself how they could modify their software to meet the company's unique needs. He discovered a few changes that would drastically increase the value of their service to the client. He pushed his recommendations upstream. They pushed back. He pushed harder. He convincingly presented his case to his superiors. The company shifted their product, the client re-signed with their company, other companies signed the dotted line, and he made multiple years' salary *in one year*. It pays to be curious!

6 SIMPLE WAYS TO START MAKING DISCOVERIES EVERY DAY

Discovery is the antidote to information addiction. You discover things when you believe that there is something to be found and are curious enough to look. Here are some ways to be intentional about making discoveries now.

1. **Block out time to observe regularly**
   Block out 10 minutes to ask, "What inflection points am I noticing?

2. **Keep an observation journal**
   Have a journal in your bag or on your desk where you can jot down observations as they come up throughout your day.

3. **Schedule reflection time**
   Daily Spend 15 minutes reflecting on discoveries.

   Weekly Spend 1 hour a week reflecting on discoveries.

   Monthly Spend 1 day a month reflecting on discoveries.

   Yearly Plan 1 overnight getaway to reflect on discoveries.

4. **Discovery walks**
   It's helpful to take short walks to observe and reflect. Moving around helps get your thoughts moving.

5. Ask open-ended questions

Use open-ended questions to
unlock discoveries.

6. Invite others into the conversation

- Engage with a coach.
- Share observations and reflections with
  colleagues or team for engagement.
- Share with a spouse or close friends.

Chapter 4

FROM DISCONNECTED TO CONNECTED

—

SOME TRAJECTORY SHIFTS IN YOUR LIFE ARE SO SIGNIFICANT THAT YOU CAN ONLY USE WORDS LIKE TRANSFORMATION TO DESCRIBE THEM. I was in a season of change where it was time to go from *Curtis v3.0* to *Curtis v4.0*. I asked myself the same questions you should ask yourself: Who am I? And where do I want to go?

This season led to multiple breakthroughs. Breakthroughs in my professional life. Breakthroughs in how I engage with my emotions and desires. Breakthroughs in how I view others and the world around me. The most significant breakthrough was a deeper connection with myself.

Breakthroughs abound when you are connected to your identity. Three common identity myths leave you feeling disconnected. When you reject these myths, you can embrace your self-worth and live a connected life.

THE 3 IDENTITY MYTHS

Myth 1: You are what you do

I just finished my first session of the pilot Breakthrough Group. It went as good as I could have imagined, yet I felt exhausted. This was abnormal for me. Over the years of coaching individuals and groups, I have built the emotional resilience for these interactions. Plus, it was my first meeting in the morning. It wasn't at the end of a long day of work. Something was different about this exhaustion, and I knew I needed to pay attention. Later in the day, I felt a deep sense of emptiness. This emotion felt so stark in light of my incredible group experience that morning. It was hard to describe. Something was happening, and I knew I had to reflect on it. I spent some time processing what I felt and why. I invited my wife and a few others into the conversation to process it with me.

Here is what I concluded. The launch of these Breakthrough Groups was a culmination of my personal and professional life for over a decade. I realized that I was conflating what I do with who I am. It was easy to do this because so much of this group was an extension of who I am. It was indeed an authentic expression of myself. But I needed to hear what I often communicate to others: *You are not what you do.* I felt the exhaustion and emptiness that results when you derive your identity from *what you do.* I needed to let go, open my hands, and stop clinging to *what I do* to answer the question, *Who am I?*

Let's be honest. This is challenging. When you are at an event, the first question you get asked is often, "What do you do?" as if that's an appropriate stand-in for "Who are you?" It's the standard operating procedure to think *what you do* is *who you are*, or worse, to think what you failed to do is a reflection of who you are.

When your identity is defined by *what you do*, your value is determined by *what you do*. It's easy to start defining your worth by whether you are succeeding or failing. Intermingling the two makes successes and failures feel like a roller coaster. When you are succeeding, you may feel self-worth. When you are failing, it's harder to feel your self-worth. In my story above, I even felt an emptiness when succeeding because I used this myth as an identity marker. This is a roller coaster you do not want to ride, yet many of us have a season pass!

Myth 2: You are what people say

Sue was a self-described people pleaser. It kept her up at night. She let what people say or didn't say affect her mood, actions, and self-worth. Her thoughts, emotions, and actions were often a reaction to what people said about her. She was over the moon when people said positive things. When people were critical, she constantly replayed the conversation in her head and sometimes lost sleep over it. It affected her mood and caused her to act in ways to prove people wrong. Sue was answering the question *Who am I?* with *what people say*.

I asked her, "What do you need to let go of to become the strategic visionary leader you want to be?"

Her response: "I need to hand off training to another director. I need to let Bob lead our store launches and hand off the facility work to someone else." Then she paused and said, "I need to let go of trying to prove that I am enough." You could divide our coaching relationship into two parts: before and after that discovery.

When she let go of the need to prove herself, she started to delegate more operational tasks. She began to have courageous conversations with colleagues. She began operating as the strategic, visionary leader she always wanted to be. All this happened because she stopped answering the question *Who am I?* with *what people say.*

Myth 3: You are what you have

Net worth is not self-worth. People are quick to say, "Not me! I don't do that." But I often see I am *what I have* veiled as the desire for financial freedom. Tom said just that, "All I want is financial freedom." His life was plagued with frustration and anxiety that resulted from what he claimed he lacked. It created turmoil in his marriage, and he felt trapped in his job.

We explored the story he was telling himself. We uncovered a negative narrative: "We are where we are because of me. I messed up along the way." This negative self-image made him defend his value in destructive ways with his wife and stripped him of his personal agency in his work life. I asked him, "What's a different story you can tell yourself about your perception of financial freedom?"

He told me he had a fantastic home in a great neighborhood. His kids are in an incredible school district. They both drove great cars. They go on vacations when they want. He has free time to pursue other interests outside of work, etc. Essentially, he went on at length to describe his financial freedom! Tom was sharp enough to realize what was happening.

His angst wasn't about financial freedom or the lack thereof at all. He was answering the question: *Who am I?* with *what I have.* When you do this, nothing is enough because *what you have* can never satisfy the question *Who am I?*

It brings turmoil into your relationships and your vocations, the very things you are seeking financial freedom to enjoy! Once you detach your personal value from what you have, you can begin to experience breakthroughs in your relationships and vocation.

You are *not* what you do.
You are *not* what people say.
You are *not* what you have.

These myths are ingrained into you. Deep down inside, you know these myths. It's time to stop believing them and embrace your self-worth.

EMBRACE YOUR SELF-WORTH

My journey of embracing my self-worth started in a stairwell! I was on a two-day retreat where I was reflecting on my life and thinking about the year ahead. I was walking up a stairwell to go up to the second floor. A framed picture caught my attention. It was a picture of Jesus being baptized by John the Baptist with these words underneath:

> *"You are my son, whom I love; with you, I am well pleased."*

It was a picture of Jesus embracing his identity as God's son, embracing God's love, and embracing God's pleasure over him.

My inflection point was as clear as day. God is speaking the same thing over me. It was time to embrace my identity as God's son in a deeper way. It was time for me to embrace God's love and pleasure for me. I meditated on these words daily for a year. It seeped into me, and now it's my reality. I am God's son. He loves me so much. He is so pleased with me. The question of my self-worth has been fundamentally answered. Whenever I sense I am answering the question *Who am I?* with *what I do, what people say, or what I have,* I know I need to return to the source of my self-worth.

Some clients derive their self-worth from family or a few close relationships. Brené Brown famously said that she has a 3x5 card in her purse with the names of the people who genuinely care for her as a person and whose opinions matter to her. She can lean into those who truly love her when she feels her self-worth is being threatened.

Others feel a deep sense of self-worth when they spend time in nature. I know someone who feels the most connected to himself on a trail with a backpack and tent. When he is away from all the noise, he feels most connected to himself.

The ramifications are endless when you embrace your self-worth:

- Your personal value is absolutely secure.
- You no longer have to prove anything.
- You no longer have to validate your self-worth through *what you do, what people say,* or *what you have.*
- You can spend your energy answering other questions because the question of your value has already been answered.
- You can trust that there are resources, opportunities, and relationships available for you.
- You can live in a place of freedom rather than anxiety.

- You are able to act courageously because the greatest fear about risk has been removed, namely, that failure or success is a reflection of your personal value.

Embracing your self-worth shifts your trajectory. Emma, Director of Marketing for an international company, described her discovery this way: "I feel free. Since I am confident in my self-worth, I no longer have to hold back who I am in my personal and professional relationships out of fear. I am showing up as my authentic self with my team, colleagues, and customers. I am speaking up where I haven't before. I am presenting innovative ideas instead of holding them back. I receive constructive criticism about how I can grow and develop positively, rather than a slight on my personal value. People have told me how my freedom has enabled them to do the same. I don't want to go back. I want this to be my new normal." In short, Emma is describing how embracing her self-worth has led to multiple breakthroughs.

What would it do for you if you embraced your self-worth?

LIVE AND WORK FROM YOUR VALUE, NOT FOR IT

Once you embrace your self-worth, you can live and work from your value, not for it. Just imagine what your life would be like if you began to live and work from your value.

- Your critical voice inside your head would become a compassionate voice.
- You would take risks because failure has lost its bite.
- You would charge what you are worth.
- You would set goals that align with who you are.
- You would ask how you can bring value to your relationships rather than extract it from them.
- You would set boundaries that honor your value.
- You would go from proving your value to bringing your value.
- You would feel the freedom to go for it! Whatever *it* is!

BE MORE YOU, NOT LESS

Once you embrace your self-worth, you feel permission to be you. We need you to be more you. Since you have immense self-worth, the more you are yourself, the more value you bring into the world. The less yourself you are, the less value you bring. Please, be you! I want to live in a world where everyone brings their full value into it.

Individuals and organizations often ask, "How can I be more like X?" Please stop! Start asking, "How can I be more myself? How can we be more us?" The more you can self-define as organizations and individuals, the more value you bring. Economics 101: If you are completely differentiated from everyone else, then you have no competition and, thus, are extremely valuable. Simply, it pays to be you. The most valuable thing you can do is be and act like yourself.

Embracing your self-worth naturally leads to an abundance mindset. It helps you trust that opportunities, resources, and relationships are available to help you succeed.

Chapter 5
FROM SCARCITY TO ABUNDANCE
—

AN ABUNDANCE MINDSET IS TRUST. A SCARCITY MINDSET IS DISTRUST. David left his corporate job to pursue his dream of taking his SEO consultancy full-time. It came from a desire to align his work life with his passion. He stepped out of the boat of certainty into the unknown. If you have ever taken courageous risks like this, you know how it feels: exhilarating, scary, exciting, anxious. Whether it is a vocational risk, a relationship risk, or anything in between. The imagined future you envision compels you to move forward, even when you may be uncertain about the next step. David was in a space filled with uncertainty. The space between what was and what's next.

Have you ever been in a space like this? You feel compelled to create something, pivot your business, pitch that new product, take that promotion, go to counseling, enter a new market, make a significant vocational shift, or move cities, but you are uncertain about the future. You have just enough courage to start. Then, you catch your breath and begin to feel the uncertainty of the space you are in.

Uncertainty can feel like a weight too challenging to bear. The weight can be immobilizing. The weight causes you to question whether this is even the right direction. The weight makes you anxious. The weight keeps you feeling stuck. You feel like you can't remove the uncertainty of the situation; therefore, you fear you will never be free of the weight.

The weight you feel is not uncertainty; it's distrust. Distrust causes you to question whether there are opportunities, resources, and relationships out there to help you. Trust chooses to believe that they are there. Scarcity is heavy. Abundance is light. As it turns out, whether you believe those things are scarce or abundant, *you're right*.

Choosing to trust unlocks opportunities, resources, and relationships that are waiting for you. If you trust this, it encourages you to look. If you distrust this, you won't look. Who will have a better chance of accessing resources, relationships, and opportunities? The one who seeks or the one who does not? The one who trusts or the one who does not? Choosing to trust can make all the difference. Will you cling to distrust, or will you choose to trust?

OVERCOMING SCARCITY

You like to tell yourself all the reasons to distrust because it justifies your scarcity mindset and helps you make sense of your lack of breakthroughs. You have failed before. Why try again? Others have let you down.

Why trust again? You lack resources. Why believe that there are resources out there for you?

You lose when you cling to distrust. It locks you out of relationships, opportunities, and resources. Trust is the key that unlocks the door.

Trust Relationships

There are people out there who want to help you win. My desire to be a coach started with Jonathan, my coach mentor. I left each conversation thinking, "This guy is all about me. He genuinely believes I can succeed. He'll do anything in his power to help me win." And he has. He has been a part of my coaching journey since the beginning. He helped open doors. He connected me to opportunities and resources. He helped me succeed.

When I left my stable job to go full-time into coaching, I emailed a handful of people asking if they knew anyone who had an office space available for me to use. A friend responded immediately. He generously let me use an office space at his building.

When I was at the beginning stages of this book, David offered to serve as my writing coach. He was a past client. David was a published author. He wanted to help me succeed. I hired him. What you are reading now is the result of that trust.

I've lost count of the people, opportunities, and resources I have been connected with because I chose to trust. My life and work are a product of the generosity of others. If you want this, you must trust relationships. When you do, it gives you the boldness to ask. When you do, it gives you the humility to receive. When you do, it gives you the courage to step out because you know you are not alone.

Trusting Opportunities

There are opportunities out there for you if you start moving towards them. Don't wait for a chance to present itself before moving towards it. Start moving towards opportunities now. Once you start moving towards them, opportunities present themselves.

Ken is a national leadership coach, speaker, and writer. He coached leaders through various professional and organizational issues. During a coaching session, Ken told me that if he could do anything, he'd focus exclusively on speaking, writing, and coaching leaders through leadership crises and into leadership convergence. He could have played it safe and stayed in general leadership coaching, where he was making a fine living. Or he could start moving towards his greatest passion and impact. He chose to trust opportunity and lean forward. He rebranded himself at 65 years old!

In our coaching relationship, he built the Legacy Leadership Group framework. It focused entirely on Leadership Crisis and Convergence through speaking engagements, writing, and coaching. Ken's laser focus caught the eye of a national organization called Nothing is Wasted, which shared his passion. Eighteen months ago, it felt like a step into the unknown. Now Ken is in his dream role with Nothing is Wasted and spends his days speaking, writing, and coaching leaders through crisis and into convergence.

Don't wait for opportunities to present themselves before moving forward. You'll be waiting for a long time! Trust that they will present themselves as you move forward. So start moving!

Trusting Resources

There are ample resources out there for you, but you will never find them if you don't start digging.

Ben is a successful VP at an international company with a yearly revenue of almost $1.2B, and he had never negotiated his salary in his professional career. I asked him, "What has kept you from doing so?" He responded, "I come from a family where you keep your head down and work hard. You don't draw attention to yourself. You let others recognize the work you have done. Negotiating my salary seems ungrateful." This story that he was telling himself kept him from accessing the resources available. In our coaching relationship, he let that story go and chose a different one.

He brings tremendous value that merits compensation commensurate with the value he provides, and it wasn't ungrateful to negotiate for it. This new story gave him the courage to negotiate his salary. He asked the COO if they could review his compensation. He met with an HR colleague within his network to discuss productive ways to engage the conversation. Ben initiated a compensation review. He dramatically increased his income and has since received two promotions. He gained more than money. His courage to advocate for himself, his team, and his company grew. He no longer saw healthy advocacy as ungratefulness but as using his power for good.

Operate as if resources are waiting to be found.

DEVELOPING ABUNDANCE

Developing abundance requires two things: *letting go* and *leaning in*.

Letting Go

First, we must let go of the distrust we are clinging to. Earlier in my career, I was betrayed by a friend who brought me into an organization. I found my footing and felt like I was rising in the organization. The next thing I knew, I was in the CEO's office getting ripped apart while my friend silently sat beside him. I felt shredded inside. It left me disoriented. We had spent a good deal of time in each other's homes. Now this. She did confess years later that she intentionally hurt me for her own professional gain. But it's one thing to hear that; it's another to let go. I was losing twice. I lost when I was in the CEO's office that day. I was losing when I allowed distrust to shape how I approached my relationships.

I remember the day I finally let go like it was yesterday. It was 5 am on a Sunday. I was sitting in a recliner, feeling all the weight of not letting go. I wrote a 5-page letter addressed to no one. I poured out everything, and I finally let it go. I took my part time coaching practice full time that the same year. It's not a coincidence. Letting go opens us up to lean in.

I had to let go of a painful relationship to open myself up to new relationships. Ken had to let go of a good opportunity for a great one. Ben had to let go of a story that kept him from accessing resources.

What do you need to let go of? Is it a past event, a painful relationship, a past failure, a limiting belief, a false narrative you are telling yourself, or something else? You know what you need to let go of. It's time to let it go so that you can lean in.

Leaning In

Leaning in is the act of choosing to trust. Leaning into relationships, opportunities, and resources.

- · I leaned in when I went all in with my coaching practice.
- · David leaned in when he left corporate America to start his own thing.
- · Ken leaned in when he narrowed his focus.
- · Ben leaned in when he initiated a compensation review.

I have seen countless people choose to lean in, which led to trajectory-shifting breakthroughs. Now it's your turn. Where do you need to lean in?

Don't let distrust weigh you down. Start trusting today to unlock the opportunities, resources, and relationships waiting for you.

Leaning in often means living into a new story. In the next chapter, we will talk about leaning into stories that bring freedom while casting off stories that bring anxiety.

Chapter 6

FROM ANXIETY TO FREEDOM

—

THE STORIES WE CHOOSE TO LIVE IN DRIVE OUR ACTIONS. *The cost isn't worth it. You will lose what you have. What if it backfires? It will ruin your relationships. Be seen, not heard. Hunker down and just be thankful for what you have. It's safer to be stuck.* This is just a small sample of the hundreds of thoughts that ran through Nicole's head on a daily basis. But you would never know.

Nicole was the Director of Inclusion and Diversity at a Fortune 200 company. She catapulted in her career for over two decades. Now, she sat at the executive table, but speaking up terrified her. Harvard even asked her to speak at an event, and she turned them down.

The tension inside her was both exhausting and crippling. She had so much to say but held much of it back. On the outside, it looked like she was making it. On the inside, her internal voice was paralyzing. Nicole was faced with three options. Two options would lead to further anxiety. The third option would bring freedom.

OPTION 1: LIVING IN THE STORY YOU HAVE BEEN GIVEN

The stories you choose to live in shape the way you show up at work and in life. You will default to the stories you have been given unless you intentionally choose to live into a new story.

Nicole was living in a story that her father gave her. He was a janitor who worked for every penny he got to keep his family fed. She respected her father for that. Yet he instilled into her at a young age, "Know your role, keep quiet, do your job, and don't mess it up." Nicole broke down barriers. She is often the only minority woman in meetings. Yet, when she goes home for Christmas, this story is reinforced by her father, "You made it beyond your station. Be thankful, and don't do anything to mess it up." She was in a position of power where she could enact change. She had much to say, yet she often remained silent because of the story she had been given. This tension was creating turmoil in her.

There is pressure to live in the stories that we have been given. These stories come from different places. They can come from a parent, a boss, yourself, your friends, your past, your partner, or somewhere else. Living in stories you have been given generates anxiety and holds you back from the life you want.

What story have you been given that you are choosing to live in? Where did that story come from? How does it make you feel? What is it holding you back from? Is it propelling you towards or keeping you from the life you want?

OPTION 2: ESCAPING THE STORY YOU HAVE BEEN GIVEN

Nicole often daydreamed of just getting out. If she left everything she built over the last two decades, maybe she'd be free from the anxiety she felt. When you feel stuck, sometimes you feel your only two options are to remain in the story you are given or escape it.

Escaping your story might temporarily relieve your anxiety, but it doesn't take it away. It often increases it. Escaping doesn't always mean leaving your role. You escape when you stop bringing your whole self to your work and closest relationships. You escape when you start leaning back instead of leaning in. You escape when you begin to use food, work, or entertainment to cope with your anxiety. You escape when you ignore the person you need to have a crucial conversation with. You escape when you keep pushing down the dream in your heart. Everyone has their own ways of escaping.

Yet escaping doesn't help. You may escape temporarily, but your anxiety is still there, even increasing. You may have escaped, but you are still stuck. Good news! There is a third option that leads you to freedom.

OPTION 3: LIVING YOUR STORY

One of the most freeing things you can do is start living your own story. Your life stops being a reaction to internal anxiety or external pressure. You begin to propel the life you want forward. Option 3 feels challenging initially because we have been choosing Options 1 or 2 for so long. Actively living your own story becomes an upward spiral that gets easier as you do it.

Nicole was exhausted from living in the story that was given to her and seeking to escape it. Throughout the coaching relationship, we began to discover what kept her silent. She uncovered the story that was given to her by her father. She found the fears that kept her quiet. She arrived at the core issue: She lost belief in the value of her own voice. She was ready to believe again!

Nicole courageously began to name and face the story given to her. She faced her fears. The pivotal moment was when she had a conversation with her father, where she accepted the man but rejected the story. The maturity to do both still amazes me. She began to use her voice in ways she never dreamed of before. She spoke up in executive meetings. She engaged with her team differently. Our last coaching session was packed with celebration as we debriefed all the breakthroughs she made. I asked her, "What will you do the next time Harvard asks you to speak?" She said, "I am going to say yes!"

REACTION/REGRET CYCLE

Anxiety is the cycle of reaction and regret. Choosing Options 1 or 2 keeps you in this cycle. When Nicole kept silent in important meetings, she was living out of the story she was given and would often regret it. She would spend the rest of the night thinking of everything she wished she had said. This regret would create further anxiety, which she would react to, and the cycle would continue.

Remember Ben from the last chapter, who never negotiated his salary in his professional career. Ben realized he was living out of a story he was given, claiming that negotiating a salary is an ungrateful act. He discovered that *not* negotiating his salary made him ungrateful, and he has regretted not doing it over his career.

Nicole and Ben realized they must live and act from their own story to break the cycle.

ACTION/SELF-BELIEF CYCLE

Freedom is the cycle of action and self-belief. Choosing to live your story breaks the cycle of reaction and regret. Choosing to live your story creates a cycle of action and self-belief. Both reinforce the other. Acting from your story increases your self-belief. And your self-belief encourages more courageous action. When you enter into this cycle, you experience freedom.

- You act rather than react.
- You show up rather than hide.
- You become more you, not less.
- You act from self-worth and with self-confidence.
- You're free.

Nicole felt free when she started using her voice. Ben felt empowered after he negotiated for what he was worth. You can feel free once you start living from your story.

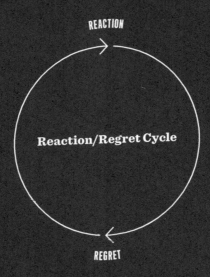

REACTION

Reaction/Regret Cycle

REGRET

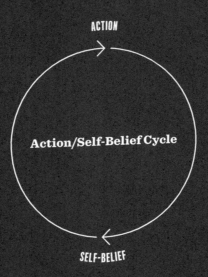

ACTION

Action/Self-Belief Cycle

SELF-BELIEF

HOW TO START LIVING YOUR STORY

1. Name the story you've been given

Naming the story helps you dissolve it of its power.
What story have you been given that you are living in?
Who or what gave it to you? How does it make you feel?
What is it holding you back from? Is it propelling you
towards or keeping you from the life you want?

2. Face it, don't escape it

Now that you have named it, it's time to face it. One
way I have seen clients face their stories is to reflect
on them. Observe how it has affected you. What has living from it cost you? Acknowledge the ways you have
been living in that story and giving it power over you.
Consider what would happen if you lived from a different story.

3. Let it go

You regain power when you let go of the stories that
do not serve you. All my best coaching relationships
involve some element of letting go. I have seen clients
let go of false stories about their identity, stories they
received from their childhood, stories they received
from their workplaces, and even false stories they have
given themselves. It often serves as the turning point
of our coaching relationship.

4. Discover your story

Letting go of unhelpful stories makes it easier for us to say, "This is who I am, and this is what I want." Once you discover your authentic story, you can begin to live from it confidently.

5. Act from it

You recover your personal agency when you start acting from your own story. Life is no longer happening to you. You are happening to life. You go from being in the passenger seat of your life to being in the driver's seat.

Breakthrough action occurs when you start to live from your story and believe in what's possible. The next chapter will show you how to increase this belief, which paves the way for courageous action.

Chapter 7
FROM INACTION TO ACTION
—

YOUR ACTIONS RARELY EXCEED WHAT YOU BELIEVE IS POSSIBLE. When you believe something is impossible, you rarely act. When you believe something is possible, it empowers you to act.

Action is ultimately a belief issue. If you want to shift from inaction to action, you should ask yourself: "What do I believe is possible?" and "Do I believe *I* can do *that?*" Increasing your belief leads to action. And action leads to breakthroughs.

"What is your greatest possible imagined future?" is one of my favorite questions. It helps me know what you believe or at least what you want to believe.

Sam's desired future was to work two days a week as the CEO of his manufacturing company so he could pursue other opportunities. Yet, it was hard for him to believe how this was possible. Over the last 20 years, he helped turn a side gig into a national company, and he wondered how the company would fare if he played a more limited role. Whether he acted on this desire was not a tactical issue but a belief issue. Does he believe he could be a two-day CEO *and* have a thriving company?

What do you think is possible in your personal and professional life? What is possible in your company or your team? If your answer is not much, I can tell you right now how much action will take place. If you genuinely believe that something is possible, your actions will reflect that.

I had the table of contents for this book sitting on my computer drive for three years. It wasn't until I believed that I could write a book that I started writing. It wasn't a content issue. I knew what I wanted to say. It was a belief issue. At a fundamental level, I needed to answer: "Can *I* do *this?*" If you are honest with yourself, the answer often is "No." Lack of belief halts significant action more than anything else. Do you believe that *you* can do *that?* Whatever *that* is!

Your actions will not exceed the level of your belief. If you believe you can, you will try. If you don't believe you can, you probably won't. I want you to believe deeply in what's possible.

EMBRACING BELIEF

Embracing belief leads to action. Action is the culmination of the 5 shifts:

1. Information to Discovery
2. Disconnected to Connected
3. Scarcity to Abundance
4. Anxiety to Freedom
5. Inaction to Action

Your belief in what's possible will increase as you progress through the first four shifts.

Embrace Discovery

Sam's coaching relationship began with goals focused on his company. Yet, he discovered aspirations to help other companies thrive and be present during critical years in his children's lives. He recognized a deep desire to take a step back and commit no more than two days a week to his company so he would have the bandwidth to pursue his other aspirations.

Sam wanted to become a fractional integrator and owner of other companies. He wanted to make this shift, but seeing how this could be possible was hard. That discovery began a journey for him. The first step he committed to was allowing himself the permission to dream about what's possible.

Discovery increases your belief in what's possible. One of the deepest discoveries you can make is answering the question, "What do I really want?" No question has stumped more clients than this one. Give yourself permission to answer this question. Your answer will open up so many possibilities for you.

Embrace Freedom

Sam is the most loyal person you will ever meet. He is dedicated to his family, friends, and company. Sam felt a tension between his desire to be a two-day CEO and his loyalty to the company. We began to unpack this tension in our coaching relationship. Sam discovered that the story he was living in was a story of duty. This story captures it best: The day after his child's birth, he went to a leadership retreat that he helped plan. His wife said he was stupid for going. Yet he felt the duty to attend.

The importance of duty was instilled into him at a young age by his father, who started a business from scratch that served his community. It was the source of his loyalty, but it also kept him from considering what he wanted. This story of duty made him feel that loyalty to his company and his desire to be a two-day CEO pursuing other opportunities were at odds. Duty trumped desire. He realized he had to detach duty from loyalty and replace it with desire. Sam realized he could let go of the story of duty without relinquishing his loyalty. This gave him the freedom to pursue his desire.

What story are you holding onto that is creating tension inside you? How can you name it, let it go, and choose to live in a new story?

Embrace Abundance

You increase your belief in what's possible as you lean into relationships, resources, and opportunities.

Sam began to lean in. He began to share his desires to be a two-day CEO and an integrator with other companies with key relationships, including his business partners and spouse. Saying it out loud made it feel more real. He began to engage with books and resources created by others who have made a similar shift in role.

Sam began to trust that there was someone out there who could fulfill the responsibilities of his role. That trust led him to someone he thought could grow into the role. They started conversing about what it could look like to take some of the responsibilities off Sam's plate.

Sam stopped waiting for the perfect moment to inform others about his desire to be a fractional integrator and owner in other companies. He told a fellow business owner and mentor about this desire and to look out for companies interested in his services. Two months later, he received a call from that same person who wanted Sam to be a fractional integrator for his company! He submitted a proposal and he landed his first high-end client.

The more Sam leaned in, the more this seemingly unrealistic dream became a genuine reality.

Embracing abundance and leaning in helps you begin to turn your desires into reality.

Embrace Self-Worth

When you embrace your self-worth, you no longer have to turn to *what you do, what people say, or what you have* for your validation.

Sam realized that a part of him was still deriving part of his self-worth/identity from his role in his company for the last 20 years. The company was "his baby." He knew he had to let go of his role as a source of his personal validation to move forward with his desire. He desired to embrace all of his self-worth outside of his position at his company. For him, this meant leaning further into his faith and family. Cutting the remaining strings that tied some of his personal worth to his role freed him up to pursue a new role. No strings attached!

Embracing your inherent self-worth takes all the stakes off the table. You no longer need to validate yourself through *what you do, what people say, or what you have* because your worth is already validated. You no longer need to prove anything. You can expend all of your energy answering other questions. You can live in a place of freedom because the question of value is already answered. You can act courageously because the greatest fear about risk has been removed, namely, that failure or success is a reflection of who you are.

YOU DON'T NEED IT TO HAPPEN

I want you to arrive at a place where you don't *need it* to happen. Whatever *it* is! Once you detach yourself from *needing* the result, it frees you to pursue it. Failure loses its bite. The stakes are removed.

When I left the security of my full-time job to pursue my coaching practice, I wrote my wife a letter. Here's the first line: *We already have everything we need.* We had a home, each other, and our son. I had made considerable strides in the five shifts in different areas of my life. We already have the things that genuinely bring contentment. At that moment, I did not *need* it to work out, which gave me the freedom to pursue it. If I start feeling anxious about needing something to happen, I need to take a step back and realize I already have everything I need. And that contentment drives my action.

Once you give up the need for something to happen, it gives you the freedom to pursue it.

BREAKTHROUGH ACTION

When you are on the cusp of a big breakthrough, it often tests your belief. You start to wonder if this is really possible. Am I the right person to do this? Will relationships, resources, and opportunities be there as I move ahead? I still feel this when I am on the cusp of action. This is a crucial juncture in the Breakthrough Circle. Will you lean back or lean forward at this precise moment? This choice will make all the difference. Leaning forward and taking that next step is an act of faith.

Faith is trust amid uncertainty. It is taking action when the future isn't clear. It takes faith to put yourself forward for a role that is not on the org chart. It takes faith to recommend an idea that changes the product or service your company is selling. It takes faith to have a crucial conversation with a colleague. It takes faith to start that company or share that idea. It takes faith to look at the world through the eyes of discovery. It takes faith to embrace your self-worth and be yourself. It takes faith to trust that opportunities, resources, and relationships await you. It takes faith to live in a story that brings freedom. This kind of faith drives the kinds of actions that lead to breakthroughs.

It's hard to have this level of faith alone. As I step back and reflect on my breakthroughs throughout my life, I realize that all my breakthroughs have come in relationships with others. None have come in isolation. I will introduce you to two proven tools, Coaching and Breakthrough Groups, that focus exclusively on:

Making Discoveries

Taking Action

Experiencing Breakthrough

Together

Part Three

—

NORMALIZING BREAKTHROUGH

Breakthroughs can be a normal part of your life, but achieving this alone is hard. I will introduce you to two tools that can make breakthroughs a regular part of your life.

Chapter 8

BREAKTHROUGH DOESN'T HAPPEN ALONE
—

YOU CAN EXPERIENCE BREAKTHROUGHS, BUT IT IS HARD TO DO IT ALONE.

You most likely can point back to a time in your life when you had an encounter with someone that led to a breakthrough. You had a conversation with a friend that led to your next business idea. Or you engaged with a mentor that clarified your life direction. A colleague connected you to an opportunity that made your career explode. Often, it's impromptu, and you look back at these one-off moments wishing they could happen all the time.

Well, they can! All you need to do is intentionally put yourself into relationships that make these one-off conversations a regular and intentional part of your life. I will introduce two proven strategies where you can do just that: Coaching and Breakthrough Groups.

HARNESSING BREAKTHROUGH

The sun is a source of seemingly endless energy, but only recently have we been able to harness it to power our homes and cities. The abundant energy was there, but we never had a way to harness the sun's raw energy until now. It wasn't a sun issue; it's always been there.

We needed the right tool, the solar panel, to harness its power.

Breakthroughs are no different. Potential breakthroughs are everywhere. You need tools that can harness your breakthrough potential. The problem is that we often use ill-equipped strategies to do this.

We get frustrated when we expect certain strategies to yield breakthroughs when they are, in fact, ill-equipped to do so. For instance,

- Conferences
- Meetings
- Focus groups
- Workshops
- Training
- Online/in-person classes

These tools often buy into the information myth presented in Chapter 3: If you just had more information, you could make the breakthroughs you want in your life, leadership, work, or relationships. Yet you spend $3000 going to a conference, and all you have is a quote on a slide deck to show for it.

How are these working for you? What tangible Return On Investment (ROI) do you see in yourself or your company as a result of the current tools you are using? Are breakthroughs the exception or the rule?

How much resources have you invested into tools ill-equipped to lead to breakthroughs?

Jill is the Director of Leadership Development at a large international company. I was in town for an event, and we decided to grab coffee. She spoke with excitement as she told me about the engaging leadership development program her team rolled out in the company. Later in the conversation, we started to talk about coaching. She has only had one conversation with a coach five years ago. It was significant for her. I curiously asked, "What has had a greater impact on you: all the leadership development programs you have been through or that one coaching call?" Her eyes started to water, then she said, "That one coaching conversation."

COACHING

Coaching is a diluted term. When I told my adult nephew I was going all in with my coaching practice, he asked me, "Which sport?" He wasn't joking! Many organizations or leaders have different ideas when they think about coaching. What do you think of when you hear the word coach? Was it a basketball coach you had when you were younger? Was it a mentor? A boss? A consultant? An instructor?

I have noticed that people are unfamiliar with what professional coaching is and how the coaching process sparks change. Yet, when you experience it, you realize how powerful it is. You may be missing out on the power of a coaching relationship simply because you do not know exactly what it is and how it could shift the trajectory of your life. Let's pull back the curtain and talk about what coaching is, how it works, and what it can do for you.

What is Coaching?

The International Coaching Federation defines coaching as *partnering with clients in a thought-provoking and creative process that inspires them to maximize their personal and professional potential.*

Simply put, coaching is a partnership with a purpose that follows a process.

Coaching is a Partnership between you and a coach that's all about you: your goals, your imagined future, and your desires. It is a confidential relationship that allows you to make discoveries and consider actions without wondering how they might be perceived. This space gives you the freedom to focus on the discoveries, shifts, and actions that lead to breakthroughs.

Coaching has a Purpose. The purpose is your personal and professional goals. You create the goals for the coaching relationship through an intake process and an initial call. You may be used to being in environments where the goals are given to you rather than creating your goals yourself. Part of the magic of coaching is that you chart the course. Your coach is dedicated to helping you navigate your map and achieve your goals.

Coaching is a Process that facilitates discovery and action. Through powerful questions and observations, coaching helps you observe and reflect on key discoveries. The coaching process connects you to who you are and the impact you want to make. The coaching process encourages you to engage with the relationships, resources, and opportunities available. The coaching process encourages you to let go of what's not serving your purpose and lean into what is. This process instills self-belief. It helps you overcome what's holding you back and encourages action. The coaching process helps hold you accountable. The discoveries you make and the actions you take move you closer to your goals.

Coaching is not consulting. Consulting is about advice. Coaching is about discovery. Consulting gives you action steps. Coaching helps you create your own. Consulting is about the consultant using their capacity. Coaching is about expanding your capacity. It's a pet peeve of mine when people say they're a coach, but they act like a consultant. Watch out! This happens more than you might think.

How Coaching Works

Coaching is formatted for you to make discoveries, take action, and experience breakthroughs. Coaching can happen virtually or in person. A coaching relationship is usually for a defined period, whether months (i.e. 7 months) or sessions (i.e. 10 sessions). Coaching sessions can range from 30-120 min long. 55-60 min sessions are most common. Most coaching relationships begin with an intake process. This intake process helps orient you to the coaching process and begins to help you articulate what you want to accomplish in the coaching relationship. The purpose of the first call is usually to define the goals of the coaching relationship. Once the goals are defined, you begin working towards those goals. Here is the structure of a standard coach call:

Standard Coach Call

- **Action steps follow up:** How did your action steps go?
- **Define the purpose of the call:** What do you want to accomplish with this coach call?
- **Define what success looks like:** What do you want to leave this call with?

- **Exploration around the call's defined purpose:** Dynamic questions and observations that facilitate client discovery.
- **Action step creation:** What action steps are you committing to between now and our next call?

The last call in a coaching relationship debriefs your experience. You reflect on the discoveries you made, the actions you have taken, and the breakthroughs you have experienced. At this point, the coaching relationship can end, or you can commit to another round of coaching with fresh goals.

CHOOSING THE RIGHT COACH

Choosing the right coach is essential for having a productive coaching relationship. Here are some questions you should ask yourself.

1. **What is the coach's track record?** The proof is in the pudding! Has the coach you are considering significantly helped other people achieve their goals? Look for testimonials from previous clients. It is even better if you know people who have received coaching from the coach you are considering.

2. **What coaching certification does this coach have?** Ensure it's a certification from a recognized governing body such as the International Coaching Federation. This credential requires intensive training, coaching hours, and mentoring to achieve. ICF coaches must recertify every two years, take continuing education, and accrue coaching hours to recertify. Watch out! Some coaching certifications only require a name and $50. Do your research.

3. **How's your chemistry?** You connect with some people better than others. You should feel chemistry with a coach before engaging in a coaching relationship. Most coaches provide a free initial discovery call. Take advantage of it to discern whether you can work with this person.

4. **Do you believe this coach can help you meet your goals?** It's all about this question. If you believe it, go for it! If not, try to find another coach.

BREAKTHROUGH GROUPS

A Breakthrough Group is a change vehicle where you make discoveries, take action, and experience breakthroughs together. It comprises 5-7 people, and a coach facilitates it. It connects 10 times (90 min) over 5 months. The group is structured for you to make key discoveries and take courageous action in your life and work.

A recent participant described a Breakthrough Group as *a group where trust is established, and everyone is bought in and committed to growing together and encouraging each other.* The group helps you make discoveries and holds you accountable for taking action.

Breakthrough Group Benefits

- Tools and structure that unlock everyday breakthroughs.
- Prioritized space in your schedule dedicated to discovery, action, and breakthrough.
- Questions, observations, and perspectives that maximize your discoveries.
- Built-in accountability propels courageous action.
- Leverage relationships and resources of group members toward your goals.
- Sustained momentum and camaraderie that result from pursuing breakthroughs together.
- Experience a change vehicle that can be iterated in your organizations and networks.

Bill, a founder and CEO, describes his Breakthrough Group experience this way:

"My goal coming into the group was growing my company by focusing on gaining new clients. During the group time period, I doubled the number of clients (which grew revenue by 40%) and took a bold step to hire business development help that will likely double revenue in the coming 3 months. Unexpectedly, I also had a breakthrough in my marriage that came from taking the initiative to have some good conversations that felt hard during a busy time of life."

Two things separate Breakthrough Groups from most other groups. 1) It's focused. You make real progress on the things that matter in your life. 2) There is a proven structure that allows you to make discoveries and take action.

Pursuing breakthroughs with others generates momentum, creates positive peer pressure for you to do the actions you committed to, and connects you to multiple people's networks that can help you succeed at your goals.

HOW TO ENGAGE IN A BREAKTHROUGH GROUP

If you would like to learn more about Breakthrough Groups, visit:

www.curtiscarnes.com/breakthroughgroups

WILL YOU JOIN IN?

I am an evangelist for a life of breakthroughs, but I'm also a convert. Over the last decade, I have pursued inflection points, breakthroughs, and the 5 shifts in my personal and professional life. I am not planning on stopping. It's a lifelong journey for me. I want the same thing for you: a life of trajectory-shifting break-throughs. Over the last decade, I have seen countless people experience breakthroughs, and it's possible for you. But what I believe doesn't matter. It matters what you believe.

- Believe that breakthroughs are everywhere.
- Believe that discoveries are all around you waiting to be found.
- Believe that your self-worth is the starting point to a more connected life.
- Believe that there is an abundance of opportunities, resources, and relationships out there to help you.
- Believe in stories that free you to live a full life.
- Believe in what's possible, and go for it!
- Believe that there are people who want to help you pursue breakthroughs.

You can do this! All you have to do is believe it and join in.

The Breakthrough Circle
—

INFLECTION POINT

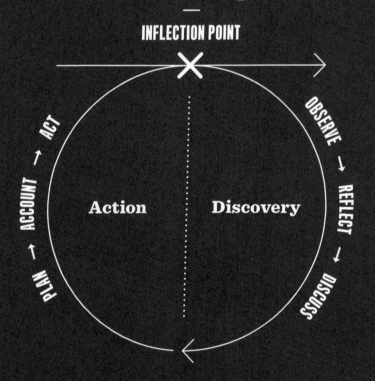

ACT

ACCOUNT

PLAN

Action

Discovery

OBSERVE

REFLECT

DISCUSS

OBSERVE

What inflection point(s) are you noticing in your life and work?

REFLECT

Take time to reflect on your discovery by asking open-ended questions.

DISCUSS

Who can you invite into the conversation?

PLAN

What action step(s) are you going to take?

ACCOUNT

What follow up question should someone ask you about your action step(s)?

ACT

Do it! Whatever it is! This is where breakthrough happens!

CURTIS CARNES COACHING

INTERESTED IN ENGAGING IN A COACHING RELATIONSHIP?

Visit www.curtiscarnes.com

INTERESTED IN ENGAGING IN BREAKTHROUGH GROUPS?

Visit www.curtiscarnes.com/breakthroughgroups

ABOUT THE AUTHOR

Curtis Carnes is an executive coach who has a decade of coaching experience. He is adept at helping leaders make breakthroughs that shift the trajectory of their professional and personal lives. He owns his own coaching practice and has created original leadership and coaching resources to train and coach leaders across the Midwest. Curtis is a Certified Coach through the International Coaching Federation. He holds a Master of Public Administration from Cleveland State University. He lives with his wife, Nancy, and son, Jay, in Cleveland, Ohio.